#NotAnotherHashtag

#NotAnotherHashtag

୬৵৹

POETRY AND PROSE OF SOCIAL INJUSTICE A BLACK MOTHER'S PAIN RAISING TWO BI-RACIAL SONS IN AMERICA

Stefanie S. Poole
James F. Carter III

DEDICATION

This book is dedicated to:

My husband, Michael, who has always stood beside me with every dream and goal I ever had.

Mommy June and Aunt Joan who have been there for me from the beginning, I would not be here if it were not for their strength and prayers to make sure I was everything I could be and am today.

My sons, Matteo and Jameson, for whom every word in this book is written. Mommy and Daddy want your lives to be protected and not harmed by all the craziness in this world merely for the skin you were born in.

My handsome stepson and beautiful stepdaughters, I love you three and pray protection over you. Just remember God will always be with you.

My aunts, uncles, and cousins who have always been there for me. I just want to thank you. Some of your stories have become inspiration for many of these poems and prose.

My best friends who have had my back and supported me through thick and thin. I love you.

My guardian angels: Grandma, Granddad, and Uncle Tuffy, thank you for always looking down and protecting us.

Finally, all of the men and women who have lost their lives senselessly to gun violence due to racial disparity and social injustice. From Dr. Martin Luther King
Jr. to Rodney King to Trayvon Martin to Eric Garner to Breonna Taylor and the list goes on. While conducting research for this book, I read that as of January 1, 2015, at least 1,252 African American people were reported to have been killed by police officers. This book was written in June 2020. Can you imagine how many more have been killed since then?

We stand for you. We think of you. We will continue to fight for you.
#saytheirnames

CONTENTS

Preface

I sat down over the years and tried to write books on my life and publish my poetry book, but nothing ever came to true fruition until now. So many things flowed through my mind and to my fingertips just naturally for this particular piece. Such raw emotions, thoughts, feelings, and words floated around. There will be some things in this book that may offend or upset certain audiences, but as one of my old pastors said, "If I hit you, I didn't mean to miss you."

The contents in this book are not intended to be child-friendly, but food for thought for all readers. If you choose to allow your child(ren) to read it or if you read it with your child(ren), please be prepared to have "the talk" with them. The talk on racism and social injustice.

How Do I?

How do I answer the questions from my sons when they ask me why?
How do I look in their faces and tell them it's ok--
When it's not?
How do I keep them protected when deep down,
I am terrified and am not really sure I can?
When I look into the eyes of Trayvon Martin
When I look into the eyes of Tamir Rice
When I look into the eyes of Michael Brown
The smiles who brightened their mothers' lives for such a short time,
Are now wings to wipe their mothers' tears.
A mother
A father
Should never have to answer the question
How?
Why?
Am I?
Will that be me?
We always want to answer – No.
But we can't
Because deep down WE are terrified
WE are not really sure WE can be there to keep them safe forever.
#YOUNGBlacklivesmatter

I Don't Fit in, Mommy

Being a black mother of two bi-racial sons and stepmother of one son in a predominantly white suburban area of Georgia is one of the most difficult situations to be in at this time in life. To have to answer questions like why are they killing Black people? Am I going to die? Hearing them name all of the white people that do like us and are not racist and have our backs should not be happening in 2020. The reality is, my husband and I are having conversations with our sons about racism and they are watching the news with us for the first time. This is our reality. The reality is not, what inventory was lost at Wendy's or Target. When I have to explain to a White lady that her daughter being ostracized by a few Black friends in her past is no comparison to what is happening to Black people today, yesterday or tomorrow. This is our past, present and I am praying to the Lord above that it is not our future.

This piece is important because it helps children to see that they are all different and it's not just their color that can make people not like them or make them feel a certain way. We need to help them see their true potential.

Mommy, who am I?
Why do I look this way?
Baby, you are who God made you to be.
In His image and the perfect you, you can be.

Mommy, I don't like this skin I'm in,
Baby, you are angelic and beautiful all on your own.
I am dark, I am not like everyone else
I wear glasses and I am smarter than most.
How can God be ok with who I am and the skin I am in?
How can I be proud of what I look like and who I am?

Mommy, this skin is no good and holds me back.
Baby, your eyes sparkle,
Your smile shines.
You have a heart of gold,
You love harder than anyone I know.
But,
Let me hear from you, I want to know what your skin does for you.
Mommy, no one likes me because of the skin I am in,
No one likes me because I know a lot.
No one likes me because I am quiet,
No one likes me because I am who I am.
You know what, mommy?
God likes me.
God loves me.
God made me.
I have a heart of an angel because God put it in me before I was formed in your womb.
I have a mind of gold because I will go far in life and fulfill the promise He has in store.
I will no longer let him, her, or them hold me back because in the end I have to make God proud of His child.
Mommy, I love me and I love who God made me to be.
#achildcanchangethings

His First Funeral

Watching in disbelief as I saw my nine-year-old son stare at my phone saddened by what is.

His first funeral.

His first funeral should be an old family member who is about 103,

Lived a long, happy, and healthy life and passed in their sleep.

He listened to the eulogy delivered by Rev. Al Sharpton who so eloquently and emphatically preached about what was, what is and what shouldn't be.

The knee on George Floyd's neck.

The knee, which metaphorically was and is the knee on the neck of the Black community.

My son sat and stared at that funeral.

His first funeral.

And he asked why.

He wrote a note on a piece of paper--

" BLACK PEOPLE SHOULD HAVE THE SAME RIGHTS AS WHITE PEOPLE! THEY CAN'T STOP US!!"

Then he looked at me confused, heartbroken, and lost with tear-filled eyes and said,

"Why do they keep doing this to us? It's not fair!"

At that point I had no words.

All I could do was hold him and let him cry.

All I wanted to do was cry.

I want to hold my babies for the rest of their lives,

Protect them from everything that could hurt them.

I wanted to protect him from watching his first funeral. But he needed to know the truth.

#cryforfairness

Close to World War III

Written By: Matteo S. Poole
From the lenses of a nine-year-old child

We need to stop this,
It's getting out of hand.
We can't have another war, especially in the United States.
Just let everyone live in peace.
We need to live in one nation under GOD.
Who cares if someone is a different skin color than you,
All that matters are their actions and their heart.
Pray for everyone during this tough time,
Please.
We all know that GOD will stop this when He knows the time is right.
Blacks are still being killed for no reason whatsoever.
It is starting to lower the Black population.
I am a Black and White child. I know that I can help the world one step at a time.
So can you. We all have a task to stop this.
#WorldWarIIICanNotHappen

Finger Pointing

Black on Black crime happens every day, but the media does not highlight it because it's just another average day in Black America.

Black on Black attacks are still occurring not ideal for the unity we as a people are trying to create.

Being told my bi-racial children should not be a part of a raising Black children group is disheartening to know it is coming from my own people,

My people.

We have been finger pointing at the police, racists, KKK, white privileged for so long.

While I am not taking anything away from segregation and racial disparity

We as African Americans do not detract from it.

When my children are not Black enough to be in a Black Facebook group because their father is White,

When they are treated this way by their own people for wanting to learn about their heritage,

How is this ok?

We spend so much time finger pointing that we forget we need to stick together.

Unity is not just a song by Queen Latifah.

The protests are not just to separate us from the police or from White people, but to create peace, to teach and to build up a community who continues to be torn down by unwarranted murder after murder.

Unjustified murder after murder.

These are not Black on Black crimes, but crimes on Black people.

Once we stop the finger pointing at other people, we will come together to make sure we as the Black, Brown, and Ally communities prayerfully have a better world for our up and coming generations as the previous generations wanted for us.

#unity

I Don't See Color

Modified from the original, written for a creative writing course in 2003.
Different times. Different meaning.

My nigga is a real nigga
A keeps me on my toes nigga
Texts me and slides in my DMs nigga
Hmmm, go figure
My nigga.
We thought we came so far using these epithets in the neighborhood. Dr.
King Jr. "freed" us from the injustice once done to our slave ancestors and
the American Indians, but guess what?

We are right back to where we were
Niggas
People of Color
Colored People
Negroes
Niggers!

We have come so far
Yet still in last place.
Come from the
Field nigga
House nigga
Street nigga
Crack nigga
Whore nigga
Lazy nigga

Nappy nigga
Dark nigga
Red-Boned nigga
Bitch ass nigga
To now, just being
My nigga?

Color does not make it ok.
So please use your words, nigga.
Upon birth,
Given a name by your placenta provider.
Each time nigga, you use nigga
Degrades.
Pale faces call you the N-word
Eight pm it's on CNN
Your brotha says nigga and it's just another nickname.
Come on nigga, be real nigga.
IT'S. NOT. A. GAME.

Men after men after men after women have died in just the last decade
for us nigga and pale bellies bounce with joy while they still collect a pension
and you, you still calling him—
My nigga!
Keep the respect WE deserve
By respecting yourself and your fellow African Americans first!
#Iseecolor

Ally

Kap took a knee and they fired him because no one stood with him.
He fought for the same thing we are fighting for now.
Justice.
Fairness.
Our lives.
Peace.
Equality.
Look to your left and right
Who is there for you when all is said and done?
Over 60 major league African American baseball players protested for Black Lives Matter
They received texts from their White counterparts in support because that was the easy thing to do.
Top headlines read—
NFL star Drew Brees recants his statement!
A repeat from four years prior related to the same BLM topic,
"I don't support with those who kneel."
Ironically, a day later, he became an ally for Black lives after much backlash.
Either you will stand with us as an ally or you will show your true colors. We don't need sympathy.
Forgiveness is a virtue that takes time to grow.

We need to forgive.
We cannot forget.
As the cameras slowly fade away
As life begins to go back to what we believe is our normal.

Our allies, true allies will be there with us,
For us
Walk by us
Cry with us
For us
Even when we can't cry for ourselves.
When it comes down to it will our allies come from behind the texts to show support to our faces?
#whoisyourally

In Loving Memory

Gun shots ring in our ears
Chokeholds round necks
I can't breathe.
Obituaries written more than papers in a freshman literature 101 class
He leaves behind his,
She leaves behind her,
I can't breathe.
Date of birth
Date of death way too close together.
There is always an excuse as to why the use of force was executed.
I thought he was going to--
I thought she had something--
I thought he was trying to--
We need to stand together as one unified force.
Black, White, Brown
Indian, Brazilian, South and North American.
We need to stop the in loving memories so we can create new memories
with THEM.
We don't need them to leave us behind.
We want them to be here to walk with us,
But they just couldn't breathe.

IN LOVING MEMORY
#dontrehamilton
#ericgarner
#johncrawfordIII
#michaelbrownjr
#ezellford
#danteparker
#tanishaanderson
#akaigurley
#tamirrice
#rumainbrisbon
#jeramereid
#tonyrobinson
#phillipwhite
#ericharris
#walterscott
#freddiegray
#altonsterling
#terencecrutcher
#philandocastile
#georgefloyd
#breonnataylor
#rayshardbrooks

Sadly, the list continues to go on
We reel for a while, but then our lives go back to business as usual.
These families will never go back to business as usual.
The trauma
The pain

The torment

How can we as a society build a community around these families?

Love them and build new memories to offset the

In Loving Memories.

#memoriestocreatememories

Serene

God grant us the serenity
Tranquil, fair, untroubled.
God grant this nation some kind of sanity
To accept the things we cannot change.
Accept things that may control us.
Why can't they accept me? Us? Together.
The courage to change the things we can
Aid those in need
We have to start somewhere.
The courage to modify what already exists
The wisdom for us to all know the difference.
Insight.
Knowledge for a lifetime
My lifetime,
Their lifetime,
All lifetime.
Know what should be changed,
Can be changed,
Will be changed.
Let my light shine.

God grant our nation the serenity—
No! Sanity,
To accept the things we will not change,
The courage to try our best,
The wisdom to know You will be there to show us the difference.
#serenity

Questions

From camera phones and security cameras
To body and dash cams.
So much evidence, but there are still questions being asked as to what happened?
I wonder if he was on drugs
I think I saw him fight back
I don't think he should have turned like that and he may not have—what?
Been murdered in cold blood?
African Americans ask, would he have been shot if he were white?
Would these questions even needed to be asked if he were white?
Would there be anything to debate if he were white?
Why are they doing this?
Why is there a double standard?
The evidence is there. The evidence is clear.
Eight minutes and forty-six seconds #GeorgeFloyd
I can't breathe 11 times in a chokehold #EricGarner
Use of unwarranted deadly force #WalterScott
One bad dude #TerenceCrutcher
**** your breath #EricHarris
This is happening while the cameras are on, but how many more are missed when the cameras are off?

Why do I have to tell my sons how to behave if stopped by the police in the future?

Why do I have to call my husband to make sure I have a witness when I am pulled over by the police?

Do you?

#unansweredquestions

Kneeling to Stand

Behavior is communication.

Pro-life rallies around our country for unborn babies waving purple flags banners and celebrating life.

Arguments have ensued since certain government officials have made it illegal for women to make a decision to have an abortion.

But men being paid millions of dollars on a football field cannot decide against honoring a piece of cloth without their livelihoods being threatened.

Behavior is communication.

Silent protests by the NBA in 2014 donning "I can't breathe," t-shirts.

Riots in 1992 in Watts.

"Open my son's casket I want them to see what they did to my boy!" Mamie Elizabeth Till-Mobley.

How far is too far?

When is this going to sink in?

Enough is enough!

Behavior is communication.

A piece of cloth is worth more than a human life?

Stand!

Hand over your heart!

ONE nation under God?

A store's inventory is worth more than a human life?

What about Target? Wendy's?

THOSE people should be ashamed are the words muttered over and over again about the rioters and protesters,

There are better ways to handle this—looting.

How?

There are better ways to handle—murdering a black man or woman in cold blood too.

Hands up—Don't shoot!

I kneel to take a stand.

#IkneelwithKap

Knees on Our Necks

I. Cant. Breathe.

Ringing over and over in my head. I could not even watch the videos in their entirety, and I can still hear them crying, see them struggling, hear them gasping.

I. Can't. Breathe.

What goes through someone's mind when they feel they need to be so harsh?

I have repeated this so many times before, but so many tears have been shed by so many mothers, children, family members, friends, and strangers.

Angry and upset because our nation, as Rev. Al Sharpton said, has its knee on our neck.

While we say, I. Can't. Breathe.

I read on social media, one White person who apparently did not understand, snidely question, "What would MLK say? He's rolling over in his grave!"

He would say, he did say, before he was murdered too, "A riot is the language of the unheard."

They have their knees on our necks.

I. Can't Breathe.

Violence is not the answer on either end, don't get me wrong. Justice needs to be served equally and voices need to be heard through the screams, the tears, pain, the hurt, the suffering.

The knees on our neck will not allow us to overcome and bring the peace to the table that we so desire.

#knowjusticeknowpeace

Separate AND Equal?

The arguments are not worth it anymore.

If I have to argue with you why our black sons, cousins, male family and friends need protection you just do not get it.

Quoting Dr. King Jr. does not make you an ally.

Remember, he was murdered fighting for the same injustice we are still fighting for today,

Smoking a cigarette at his motel.

The difference is—

There is some difference but not much,

Protests are evidence of this.

The signs.

The riots.

The anger.

The frustration.

The social media outbursts.

The angst from so many people across the nation

Sadly, not enough people because the leadership is not showing what we need to unify us as a nation to stop it.

There is a systemic problem

WE need a systemic response.

Racism needs to be addressed and people need to call it what it is.

Stop talking around it,

Stop pretending the 'R' word does not exist.

Stop asking questions like,

Well what did George Floyd do to cause this?

What happened during the shooting?

Something else must have happened that was not seen on the dash cam.

Making excuses as to why these men and women are dead because police are good people.

Racism is racism is racism

Call it what it is

The systemic problem

Needs a systemic response.

Call it out

Call them out

Stop being afraid to speak up, speak out, make a change for your, my, our BLACK children!

We are not equal and until there is change, we will covertly be   separate whether we like it, want it or not.

#equalityANDpeace

It's Not Over

Fists raised high in the air with pride and freedom
On one knee protesting rights fought for so long and by so many.
Water hoses
Tear Gas
Rubber bullets
All for what?
Because,
Black Lives STILL Matter!
When I hear, what about all lives?
I simply remind them in 2020 of the over 1,500 and counting Black lives lost since January 2015
Just for being Black,
I mean, being a threat.
The fight for equality still marches on.
As I watch the dash cam footage of Laquan McDonald
16 shots as he lay clinging to life on the ground unable to move, breathe, or speak.
12 minutes of laying handcuffed in a prone position and suffering from cardiac arrest.
That was how Carlos Ingram Lopez died.
Lopez wasn't Black. Nope.
But he was a minority, which means he was a threat, too.

For 12 minutes he suffered, and his minority-life became useless.

How many social media hounds get up in arms about Dr. King Jr. turning over in his grave for the riots?

What about Dr. King Jr. turning over in his grave for this?

The fight he fought,

Is still not over!

We will fight until the victory is won.

We will march until we are equal.

We will unite until we are heard.

Black and Brown lives STILL matter.

#itsnotover

Living While Black (LWB)

One bad apple, you finish the phrase.
This is how America refers to the police department.
There are some bad cops everywhere,
In every city,
In every precinct,
Give them a chance,
Thank a cop.
LWB, doesn't get this same grace.
LWB, all a threat.
LWB, whether a woman or man racial profiling will still happen.
LWB, still have to have the "talk" with our children regardless of age.
LWB, never get the benefit of the doubt.
LWB, must be a thug no matter of the letters behind the name.
LWB, only accepted in the Ivy League schools because they checked the African American box.
This is what happens when Living While Black.
In the American 21st Century,
What is justice?
Land of the FREE-ish
A word that keeps looming
Justice.
Just. Us.

Blacks, African Americans, People of Color, Minorities,
Alone, lonely, solo, forsaken, unattached
Unattached, but more so detached from the society in which we live.
It is time for a change from the racial disparity and to turn the just us to
JUSTICE!
No one wants to live while black anymore.
We want to just live.
#fromjustustojustice

Not at Risk

There is no guarantee how long a Black man will live after he is born.

There is no guarantee how many breaths he will take after his first.

There is no guarantee how many steps parents will count before the last step their child takes.

These are passing thoughts in my mind while raising two Black sons.

The tears are full of pain.

The tears are full of fear knowing there are no guarantees.

As I look around this town and I think about the risks my children could endure.

I pray daily for their lives,

Their safety,

That they know to just comply.

Don't run!

Don't fight!

While their father is White, they are still Black.

They ARE at risk.

So many have gone senselessly before us, whether we want to believe it is God's will or not,

God gave us free will.

Some have taken that free will and used it to become judge, jury and executioner.

As a mother, a father, a grandparent we have to make sure we teach

certain things to our children different than those of our White counterparts.

This is not where this is going to end.

We are not giving up on our children.

There is no guarantee, but we teach them the best way we know how, and we pray God will lead them the rest of the way.

Stay faithful.

Stay quiet.

Stay compliant.

Stay safe.

Stay alive.

Everyday cannot be lived in fear and shame because of the color of our skin.

Our skin color cannot be at risk day in and day out. Scratch that, our skin color SHOULD not be at risk day in and day out.

Unarmed black men should not be shot while jogging,

Suffocated to death,

Shot while peacefully intoxicated in a fast food parking lot all within a matter of 4 weeks.

What is so intimidating?

We are at risk.

When will the time come when we are not at risk? For decades it has been the quite the contrary the only difference is, we now have a stronger voice. The voice is all we have.

#stillatrisk

A Positive Light

Turning to my husband hindered by writer's block, I feel everything written is so dreary and disheartening for everyone reading.

I said, "what else can I write and how can I turn this positive?"

He said, "what positive is there to say? You have to be real. You have to be raw. You have to be honest. That's what you're doing and that is what your readers want and need to see."

As I ponder and attempt to find positivity,

To write positivity,

I struggle.

I get stuck.

I ask God for some relief and some words to break through my mind.

Everything that came to mind immediately was what had, has and is being done to all of these Black people,

All of the protests, riots, the documentaries filmed, cities destroyed, families torn apart.

It was hard to see any light.

It was hard to find the calm in the storm.

The light was to see us as people.

To see us as intellectuals, lawyers, teachers, architects, artists, dancers, chefs, writers, psychologists, friends, wives, husbands, daughters, and sons.

We are people who deserve the same love as the next man and woman regardless of race.

We are no different.

The positive light will show the creativity, sensitivity, humor, love, and humanness we exhibit.

#reachingforsomething

More Justice, More Peace

Truth and honesty. Love and respect.
Four words that are not mutual across this nation for all mankind.
Chants ringing, loudly singing,
"No justice, No peace!"
Through cities and communities in the United States flooding streets with signs of unity and support.
"No justice, No peace!"
What does this truly mean though?
The peace desired,
The peace sought for.
Because of the color of your skin, you don't have to be afraid to take a run
Because of the color of your skin, you don't have to be afraid to drive your nice car down the street.
Because of the color of your skin, you don't have to be afraid to walk through Walgreens.
Because of the color of your skin, you don't have to be afraid to leave 7-11 with a hoodie on carrying Skittles and an Iced Tea.
Because of the color of your skin, you don't have to be afraid to wear dreadlocks.
Because of the color of your skin, you don't have to be afraid to stand on your balcony smoking a cigarette.
Because of the color of your skin, you don't have to be afraid to speak up at meetings.
Because of the color of your skin, you don't have to be afraid.
Living out these truths have not been self-evident as one Dr. Martin Luther King Jr. spoke about because ALL men are created equally but being created equally and treated equally are two different mindsets.

Justice and peace are all this country should strive for.

That is what we as parents, grandparents, neighbors, and friends should desire for this next generation.

The next generation should not live in a world where they are afraid to live because they are afraid to die.

#morejusticeforusall

Black Lives Matter

Written by my husband, Michael Poole in collaboration with other artists as a hip-hop piece to celebrate Black lives and promote equality and justice in America.

On my life, thinking about my wife, tears in her eyes
Reason I cry?
My son asked if he's gonna die.
Not gonna lie, if my child had a knee to his neck
Begging to breathe, I'd want the whole city to bleed.
Take a second to breathe, not afforded to some
What do you expect?
You shoot people in the back when they run
Now they're done, not havin it
I'll play the Kaepernick, on my knees
Praying in the heavenlies, please
The passion--Reggie Noble, time for some action
Time to bring healing to the streets, reach the masses
For those that are asking, that's what the task is
Grab their hand, lead them to the Man in Damascus
Play how you practice, kinda what the track says
If you're really down, pound your fist and demand it
That's why we're standing, that's why we're chantin
In the crowd, say it loud
#BlackLivesMatter

#NotAnotherHashtag

I tried to write all these lines and make them flow word after word to appeal to everyone. Then it hit me after reading so many posts on social media and cries for help and cries for social justice and pleas for equality. Time and time again we keep piling on these hashtags when did this become a trend?

When is this going to stop?

Adding new hashtags has become like buying new Jimmy Choo shoes or the latest Jordans

Once the hype is gone everyone goes about their day and their lives.

Is this going to be just another passing trend?

Hashtag BLM

Hashtag No Justice No Peace

Hashtag Say his name

Hashtag Hands up don't shoot

Hashtag I can't breathe

This should be problematic not just for one community, but for our nation

This should be problematic not just for one state, but for our leadership

This should be problematic not just for the moment, but forever until WE as a country begin to see a change

WE should all be tired of the continued hashtags

WE should be tired of the protests

WE should be tired of the riots

WE should be tired of the division

WE should be tired of the hatred

WE should just be tired.

When will it stop?

Until there is

#notanotherhashtag

About the Author

Stefanie S. Poole graduated from Towson University in 2004 with a Bachelor of Science in Psychology and a Minor in Creative Writing. In 2013, she graduated from California Baptist University with a Master's in Education specializing in School Psychology.

As a mother, more importantly a mother of Black children, Stefanie and her husband have seen the impact of teaching equality to their children in an unequal world. Staying faithful to God and one another they will endure the storms racial of injustice while also instilling the qualities of acceptance.

CPSIA information can be obtained
at www.ICGtesting.com
Printed in the USA
BVHW020244140920
588704BV00009B/440